Dropping In On...
VIETNAM

Lewis K. Parker

A Geography Series

ROURKE BOOK COMPANY, INC.
VERO BEACH, FLORIDA 32964

A Blackbirch Graphics book.

Printed in the United States of America.

Library of Congress Cataloging-in-Publication Data

Parker, Lewis K.
    Vietnam / Lewis K. Parker.
        p.   cm. — (Dropping in on)
    Includes bibliographical references and index.
    ISBN 1-55916-008-X
    1. Vietnam—Description and travel—
Juvenile literature.   I. Title.   II. Series: Parker,
Lewis K.   Dropping in on.
DS556.39.P38   1994
915.9704'4—dc20   94-7558
                                                    CIP
                                                    AC

Vietnam

Official Name: Socialist Republic
of Vietnam

Area: 127,246 square miles

Population: 71,800,000

Capital: Hanoi

Largest City: Ho Chi Minh City

Highest Elevation: Phan Si Pan
(10,308 feet)

Official Language: Vietnamese

Major Religions: Buddhism,
Roman Catholic

Money: Dong

Form of Government: Communist

TABLE OF CONTENTS

Our Blue Ball—The Earth

The Earth can be divided into two hemispheres. The word hemisphere means "half a ball"—in this case, the ball is the Earth.

The equator is an imaginary line that runs around the middle of the Earth. It separates the Northern Hemisphere from the Southern Hemisphere. North America— where Canada, the United States, and Mexico are located—is in the Northern Hemisphere.

The Northern Hemisphere

When the North Pole is tilted toward the sun, the sun's most powerful rays strike the northern half of the Earth and less sunshine hits the Southern Hemisphere. That is when people in the Northern Hemisphere enjoy summer. When

the North Pole is tilted away from the sun, and the
Southern Hemisphere receives the most sunshine,
the seasons reverse. Then winter comes to the
Northern Hemisphere. Seasons in the Northern
Hemisphere and the Southern Hemisphere are
always opposite.

Get Ready for Vietnam

Hop into your hot-air balloon. Let's take a trip! Vietnam is in the Northern Hemisphere and is a long and narrow country in southeast Asia. It is about the size of the state of New Mexico. From the air, Vietnam looks like the letter "S." It is bordered on the east by the Gulf of Tonkin and the South China Sea, and on the southwest by the Gulf of Thailand. At its northern border is the nation of China. The nations of Laos and Cambodia touch Vietnam's western border.

Vietnam can be divided into 3 main areas. The middle area has Vietnam's large mountain range—the Truong Son Mountains. Between the mountains and the South China Sea are the coastal plains. The southern coastal plains contain the Mekong Delta, which is the largest farming region in Vietnam.

CHINA

STOP 7

Lao Cai

CHINA

STOP 6

Hanoi

MYANMAR

LAOS

Gulf of
Tonkin

STOP 5

STOP 4

Truong Son Mountains

Da Nang

THAILAND

N

W   E

S

STOP 3

CAMBODIA

Da Lat

Ho Chi Minh
City

Gulf of
Thailand

STOP 1

South
China
Sea

STOP 2

Mekong Delta

Vietnam

⭐ National Capital

0   Miles   100

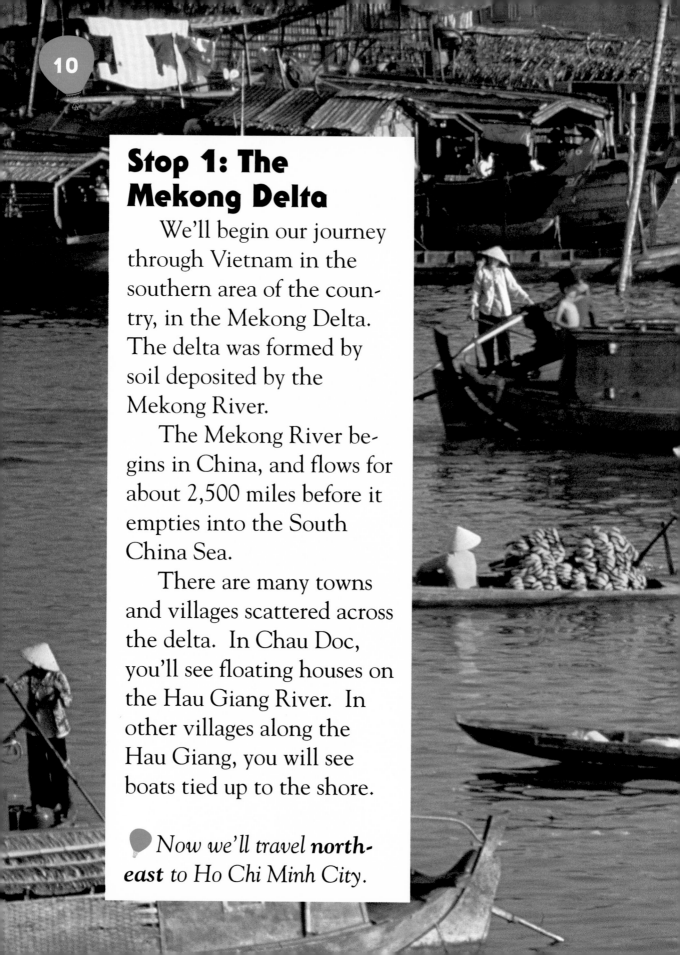

Stop 1: The Mekong Delta

We'll begin our journey through Vietnam in the southern area of the country, in the Mekong Delta. The delta was formed by soil deposited by the Mekong River.

The Mekong River begins in China, and flows for about 2,500 miles before it empties into the South China Sea.

There are many towns and villages scattered across the delta. In Chau Doc, you'll see floating houses on the Hau Giang River. In other villages along the Hau Giang, you will see boats tied up to the shore.

*Now we'll travel **northeast** to Ho Chi Minh City.*

The Mekong River is a busy route for transporting passengers and goods.

Stop 2: Ho Chi Minh City

The first things you notice about Ho Chi Minh City are that it is a large city and its streets are packed with people. More than 4 million people live here! Lots of traffic flows through this busy city. You don't see many cars, but you do see

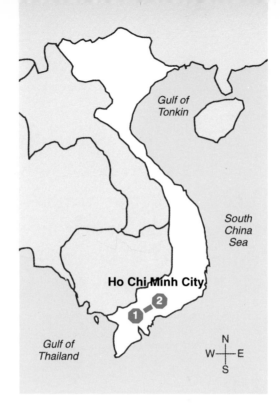

thousands of motorbikes, bicycles, and cyclos. Cyclos are like taxis—people ride in the carriages while a driver pedals.

Ho Chi Minh City has wide streets lined with shade trees. Tamarind trees are everywhere and they are easy to pick out with their red-striped, yellow flowers. Bougainvillea, a vine that has purple and red flowers, also helps to make the city glow with color. The city has buildings that are over 100 years old, and modern buildings that were built just a few years ago.

A good place to visit is the zoo. There you can buy balloons and watch elephants drink water with their trunks. You can also see black panthers and monkeys in their cages.

While we're visiting Ho Chi Minh City, you'll want to stop in Ben Thanh Market. This is the largest market in the city. The entrance to the market has an enormous gateway and clock tower. Inside, you can buy fruit, vegetables, meat, fish, noodle soup, and clothing.

You can't miss the beautiful Notre Dame Cathedral. This gigantic church was built by the French about 100 years ago. A tall statue of the Virgin Mary stands in front of the cathedral. The cathedral itself is built in a square that faces the street. It has a red brick front, stained glass windows, and 131-foot-tall towers topped with spires.

Notre Dame Cathedral has 2 beautiful spires (tapered structures that come to a point), which sit on top of the towers.

Vietnamese water puppets perform on a stage in Hanoi.

Water Puppet Shows

Only in Vietnam will you find water puppet shows. These shows are called *roi nouc* and are performed during special festivals.

People who pull the puppets' strings stand in water up to their waists. Bamboo screens keep viewers from seeing them. The puppets usually act out a legend or folktale. One of the most famous stories is about the "Golden Turtle and the Lake of the Restored Sword."

*Now we'll travel **northeast** to Da Lat.*

Da Thien Lake is surrounded by the Valley of Love. Here, you can sail on the lake or take walks through the woods.

Stop 3: Da Lat

Da Lat sits on the southern plateau in the Central Highlands. It is about 5,000 feet above sea level. High in these mountains, the air is cool and springlike. All around Da Lat are lakes and waterfalls. From Da Lat, you can see the coastline.

About 125,000 people live in Da Lat. The area is known for its farming and its flowers, such as orchids and poinsettias. Farmers grow tea, coffee, and strawberries.

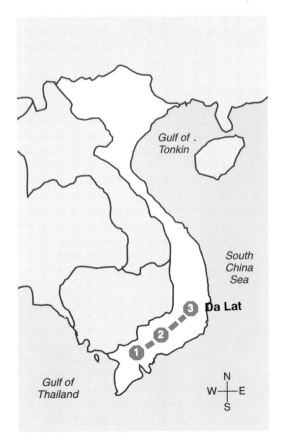

In the center of Da Lat is Da Thien Lake. Just north of the lake is the Valley of Love. This is a scenic area where you can ride horses among the trees. You can also ride in paddleboats on the lake. Or, you can take a ride in one of the big canoes that can hold 15 people.

LET'S TAKE TIME OUT

Rice paddies are flooded to prepare the land for planting and growing rice.

Rice Farming

Vietnam's rich farmland and hot climate are perfect for growing rice. However, rice is not easy to grow. It must be planted in just the right place.

When the rice seeds have grown into stalks, they are pulled up and re-planted in paddies. This is where the rice will grow and be harvested.

Water buffalo pull plows across the fields. Most of the planting is done by women.

The rice has to be kept under water. It is harvested in March and August. It is brought in from the fields to dry in the sun. When the rice is dry, it is stored in bins.

*Now we'll fly **north** to Da Nang.*

Thuy Son, in the Marble Mountains, is filled with beautiful, dramatic caves.

A child rides along the river in Hoi An.

Stop 4: Da Nang

Da Nang is the fourth-largest city in Vietnam and about 400,000 people live here.

Da Nang is famous for its marble. You may want to visit the Marble Mountains. These mountains are really 5 large marble hills. According to Vietnamese beliefs, each of the hills stands for an element of the universe— water, wood, fire, gold, and earth. The largest hill is called Thuy Son. It has many caves where Buddhist religious ceremonies are held.

About 19 miles south of Da Nang is Hoi An, a very old river town. Some parts of Hoi An look just as they did hundreds of years ago. Hoi An is famous for the cotton cloth that is produced here.

*Let's leave Da Nang and travel **northwest** to the Truong Son Mountains.*

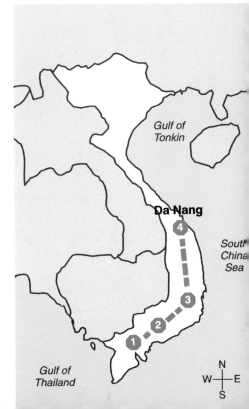

Stop 5: Truong Son Mountains

Houses are built on floating platforms on the La Naga River in the Truong Son Valley.

The Truong Son Mountains form a long chain that runs almost the full length of Vietnam. The mountains run along Vietnam's borders near Laos and Cambodia.

In the northern mountains, you will see dense forests and jungles of teak, oak, and pine trees. Animals such as panthers, elephants, wild peacocks, and monkeys live in the rainforests and jungles. More than 200 rivers flow through this area. These rivers cut very narrow valleys and make beautiful, high waterfalls.

Parts of these mountains stretch eastward to the South China Sea.

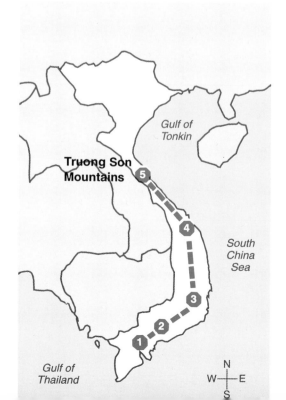

A male peacock displays its beautiful colors.

LET'S TAKE TIME OUT

Above: Children cover their ears as firecrackers explode during Tet.

Inset: Colorful dragon costumes are used as part of the Tet celebrations.

Tet: Vietnamese New Year

In Vietnam, the most important holiday is *Tet*, the Vietnamese New Year. It usually occurs in late January and lasts about a week. During this time, people visit their friends and relatives, watch parades, give gifts, and play games.

Tet is celebrated in different ways in different parts of Vietnam. Flower shows and firecracker festivals are held in some cities. People compete to see who can set off the loudest firecracker.

Boys and girls also take part in *hat doi.* This is a chorus in which the groups sing to one another.

Let's hop in our balloon and travel **north** *to Hanoi.*

Stop 6: Hanoi

Hanoi is the capital of Vietnam. It is located along the right bank of the Red River. Hanoi is a large city with almost 2 million people.

In the center of Hanoi is Hoan Kiem Lake. This lake is also called the Lake of the Restored Sword. According to Vietnamese legend, heaven gave an emperor a powerful sword. One day, the emperor was in a boat on the lake. A golden turtle grabbed the sword and disappeared into the water. Since that time, the lake has been called the Lake of the Restored Sword because the turtle returned the sword to heaven.

Another famous sight is the One Pillar Pagoda. It was built 1,000 years ago. It is made of wood and stands on a stone pillar, which is about a yard wide. It looks like a lotus blossom, the symbol of purity in Vietnam.

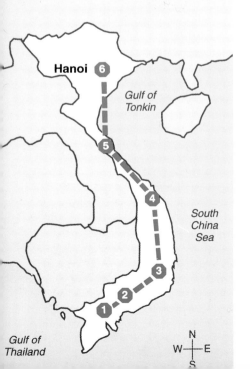

Vietnam's capital city has many old buildings and narrow streets.

The Montagnards

The Montagnards live in the Central Highlands and the mountains of the north. The word "Montagnard" is from the French language and means "mountain people" or "highlanders."

There are over 60 Montagnard tribes living throughout Vietnam. Many Montagnards are farmers. They grow crops such as coffee, tea, sweet potatoes, and dry rice. (Dry rice is rice that can be grown without being covered by water.)

*For our final stop, we'll travel **northwest** to Lao Cai.*

A Montagnard family stands outside its home.

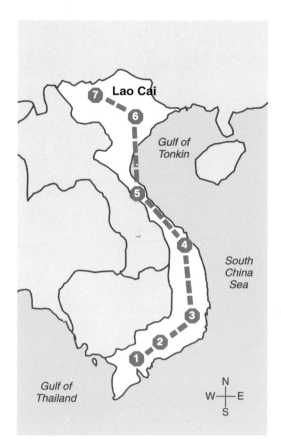

Stop 7: Lao Cai

We will finish our visit to Vietnam high in the mountains. The Hoang Lien Mountains are sometimes called the Vietnamese Alps. They are the highest peaks found in this country. The highest point is Phan Si Pan Mountain. It is 10,308 feet high.

Lao Cai is a small town, but it is the largest town in these mountains. From this high up you can see Vietnam spread out before you.

The village of Lao Cai is in some of Vietnam's most beautiful mountains.

Food in Vietnam

There are more than 500 different kinds of Vietnamese foods. Rice is served in, or with, almost all of them. Rice can be mixed with coconut, ground into flour, or made into paper that you can eat.

Different types of dishes are sold by vendors on a street in Hanoi.

Most Vietnamese food is diced up into small pieces. You eat by using chopsticks, called *duon*, to take rice from a large bowl. You place the rice into your own bowl, and then use the chopsticks to add meat, fish, or vegetables to your bowl.

Now it's time to set sail for home. When you return, you can think back on the wonderful adventure you had in Vietnam.

Glossary

Buddhism An eastern religion that originated in India.

delta An area of land formed by deposits of earth at the mouth of a river.

emperor The male ruler of an empire.

pagoda A temple or tower of several stories, often with a series of roofs that curve upwards.

plateau An area of flat land raised above the surrounding land.

spires Tapered structures that come to a point and are usually atop towers.

tribe A group of people that share the same culture, ancestry, and social customs.

Further Reading

Jacobsen, Karen. *Vietnam.* Chicago, IL: Childrens Press, 1992.

Nhuong, Nuynh Quang. *The Land I Lost: Adventures of a Boy in Vietnam.* New York: Harper Collins Childrens Books, 1990.

Wright, David. *Vietnam Is My Home.* Milwaukee, WI: Gareth Stevens, 1992.

Index

Acknowledgments and Photo Credits
Cover: ©Beziau-Boisber-Figaro/Gamma Liaison; pp. 4, 6: National Aeronautics and Space Administration; p. 10: ©Gamma Liaison; pp. 12, 16, 21: ©Noboru Komine/Photo Researchers, Inc.; p. 14: ©Joe Lynch/Liaison International; p. 15: Reuters/Bettmann; p. 18: ©Wolfgang Kaehler/Liaison International; p. 20: ©Renault-Rieger/Gamma Liaison; p. 22: ©Alain Evrard/Photo Researchers, Inc.; p. 23: ©Gregory Dimijian/Photo Researchers, Inc.; pp. 25, 28: ©Philip J. Griffiths/Magnum Photos; p. 25: ©Joe Lynch/Liaison International (inset); pp. 27, 30: ©J. C. Labbe/Gamma Liaison.
Maps by Blackbirch Graphics, Inc.